IRISH LIFE AND LORE SERIES

RECOLLECTIONS OF 1916 AND ITS AFTERMATH

ECHOES FROM HISTORY

By JANE O'HEA O'KEEFFE
Recordings compiled and edited by MAURICE O'KEEFFE

Privately published by Maurice O'Keeffe & Jane O'Hea O'Keeffe
2005

Printed by KINGDOM PRINTERS LTD.
TRALEE, CO. KERRY. *Tel:* 066 7121136

Printed June 2005

ISBN 0 9543274 4 6

*Front cover illustration: Officers of the First Southern Division, IRA, attending Army
Convention, Mansion House, Dublin, 9th April 1922, photo courtesy of George Rice.*

ACKNOWLEDGEMENTS

We wish to sincerely thank all the participants in the recordings referred to in this book for their most valuable recollections, their unfailing co-operation and patience and their generous hospitality.

This project has been substantially assisted by funds from the Department of Arts, Sport and Tourism.

We would like to thank the following historians who have generously shared their special knowledge of the 1916 - 1923 period.
Ryle Dwyer, Tralee, Michael Lynch and Eamon Browne from Kerry County Library, Fr. Anrhony Gaughan, Dublin, Russel McMorran, Tralee, Nollaig O'Gadhra, Galway and Heléne O'Keeffe, Cork.

Our gratitude must be expressed to the following people for the loan of photographs and historical material: Eddie Barrett, Frank Blennerhassett, Des and Pam Cooke, Ryle Dwyer, Jack Farmer, Michael Finucane, the late William Geary, Kathleen Kennedy, Michael Howard, Paddy Hurley, Aine Kelliher, Padraig Kennelly, "The Kerryman" newspaper, James Miller, Donal Mc Sweeney, Bridget O'Connor, the late Michael O'Leary, George Rice, Diarmuid Ring, Meda Ryan and Rory Sweeney

We must also thank Kieran Mc Carthy of Kingdom Printers for his great expertise, Nora Burke, our typist, for her patience and efficiency and Kerry Audio Productions for the professional production of the recordings

The complete collection of 30 recordings or any individual recording may be obtained
by contacting: Maurice & Jane O'Keeffe
                    Ballyroe, Tralee, Co. Kerry.
                    066 7121991
or through website: www.irishlifeandlore.com
                    email: okeeffeantiques2@eircom.net
Individual cd's: €20
Complete collection of 33 cd's: €500

INTRODUCTION

The oral heritage of Ireland is a rich and unique treasure. It envelopes cold historical fact in a warm human face. When the oral tradition is corroborated by documentary evidence, it can prove a truly invaluable source of social information and an important portal into a past long faded from view.

A sense of belonging is a fundamental necessity in all of humanity. Our own story and its telling is as vital to our sense of wellbeing as a good meal and a warm bed. Setting down our story in the context of documented historical record is a matter of integrity and some pride, and thereby an active relationship is established between the past and the present, between history and memory.

The oral tradition can sometimes carry vital information which may be incidental to the story being told, but can prove a strong historical clue to an event from the past. Though not a reliable historical source, the spoken word can be invaluable in its clear indication of the social and historical circumstances in which it is rooted.

It has been a privilege for me to work on this book "1916 and its Aftermath - Echoes from History", along with my husband Maurice O'Keeffe, who made the recordings. Each of the thirty recordings makes a fascinating oral contribution to the historical record of that troubled period in our history and we are very grateful to have been allowed access to some important primary source material not previously in the public arena.

The work has been undertaken with care as we are cognisant of the fact that without our oral tradition in all its richness of story and song, we are truly impoverished and enslaved in the cold light of the present. We, as a people, should never allow all the poetry and nuance of voice and language which constitutes our oral tradition to be neglected as it is a fragile and wonderful resource which must be preserved and honoured.

Jane O'Hea O'Keeffe
June 2005

FOREWORD

In this collection of "Recollections of 1916 and its aftermath - Echoes from History" and the accompanying book, Maurice O'Keeffe and Jane O'Hea O'Keeffe capture the atmosphere of our revolutionary period.

Those interviewed were good story-tellers. They recalled incidents which impacted vividly on their young minds and imaginations. For the most part the events they remembered were dark events.

There was the terror struck on all and sundry in Tralee and its neighbourhood by the notorious Black and Tans, known as 'Big Paddy and the Jew' in 1920-1. Then the incident witnessed by the father of Mike Christopher O'Shea. Mick O'Connell, father of the later famous footballer had to come to Caherciveen from his home in Beginish Island. As the Angelus bell began to ring he removed his cap and knelt down on one knee in the street to pray the Angelus. He was approached by two members of the Black and Tans, Coffee and Allen, and ordered to say "To hell with the pope." He refused to comply. The Tans beat him mercilessly with their rifle butts and walked calmly away.

But, as more than one interviewee acknowledged, not all members of the Crown forces were repressive. The people at Camp addressed the resident RIC as follows:
Buckley is a gentleman
Barney is a spy
Phelan is a traitor and a traitor he will die,
Not forgetting Shelbourne
And Burke is worst of all
He made the people shiver when he came from Annascaul

These interviews were conducted by Maurice O'Keeffe during the past few years and in so doing he has ensured the preservation of information which otherwise would have gone to the grave. Herein are valuable snippets of information which add colour and sometimes extra detail to well known events in the narrative of the War of Independence and its aftermath.

The book, compiled by Jane O'Hea O'Keeffe to accompany the recordings, will be of interest to local historians, students of our revolutionary period and Irish people at home and abroad.

J. Anthony Gaughan
20 May 2005

Col. Sean Clancy, Dublin

CD No. 1

Time: 78.55

Publisher: Maurice O'Keeffe. ©

During the summer of 2003, the family of Col. Sean Clancy made contact with me as they were anxious that the recollections of this remarkable man should be recorded and preserved, as he had lived through the historic and turbulent days of the early 20th century. In November of that year I made my way to Dublin and met Col. Clancy at Newtownpark Nursing Home, where he is now resident.

Sean Clancy was born in East Clare in July 1901 and recalls clearly being sent to Limerick on an errand by his father on Easter weekend 1916. The city was agog with news of something happening in Dublin, but as no newspapers were circulating nothing could be confirmed.

In 1919, he left for Dublin where he joined the Volunteers, 2nd Battalion, Dublin Brigade. He described for me in detail the mood of the people in Dublin in those troubled times. He later joined the Free State Army and worked with Michael Collins in Portabello Barracks.

Sean has a clear memory of the events of Bloody Sunday. "It was a night of terror in Dublin", following the shootings in Croke Park, he told me. As a younger man he was a loyal supporter of Eamon de Valera, but following de Valera's decision not to go to London for the Treaty negotiations in 1921, his loyalties changed and his opinion of the man was revised.

My first meeting with Col. Sean Clancy proved fascinating and vastly informative and I promised to return on another day to record some more of the recollections of this wonderful man.

Col. Sean Clancy, Dublin and his god-daughter Sr. Claire Dineen

CD No. 2
Time: 38.50
Publisher: Maurice O'Keeffe. ©

My second visit to Col. Sean Clancy coincided with his 103rd birthday and on my arrival I was met by the postman who was delivering a letter from President McAleese to mark the occasion. Once the excitement had abated we settled down to record further recollections of stirring times in Irish history.

Col. Clancy has a vivid memory of the occasion of the handing over by the British of Dublin Castle to the Irish in 1922. He attended the ceremony dressed in civilian clothes as a representative of the Volunteers and he recalls Collins arriving through the lower Castle Yard entrance in a dilapidated taxi to be met by a British officer and told he was seven minutes late, and had kept the Lord Lieutenant waiting. Collins was not found wanting in his quick witted response!

During the Civil War, Col Clancy was working with records and troop payments and in 1924 he was sent to Kerry to help with demobilisation, and he had several narrow escapes on the roads where snipers were very active.

As I was preparing to take my leave Col Clancy told me he had one last fascinating story to relate. A good friend of his John T. Moloney, a member of the IRB, was in Tralee during Easter weekend 1916, and watched as three elderly RIC officers entered the town escorting a tall upright man. He went to Austin Stack, the local IRB leader, and asked for assistance for the prisoner. Stack was adamant that no action was to be taken as he did not want any trouble in the town. The prisoner was Roger Casement who was being brought to Tralee barracks from his place of capture at Banna.

I was privileged to be allowed to record the memories and stories of a man who has played such an important role in our history and whose recollections are as clear today as one could ever wish.

Tom Barry of Kilmichael Ambush

Meda Ryan and Donal McSweeney

CD No. 3
Time: 49.37
Publisher: Maurice O'Keeffe. ©

This recording is dedicated to the life of Tom Barry and to his participation in the famed Kilmichael Ambush.

In November 2003 I travelled to the home of Donal McSweeney at Gortnafuinsion, Ballyvourney, Co Cork. This house was known locally as a meeting place for the Volunteers in the early years of the 20th century, and waiting at the house when I arrived was author and historian Meda Ryan. Meda Ryan has recently written a biography of Tom Barry and she began by telling me that he was born in 1897 and lived in Killorglin until the family moved to Bandon when Tom was 14 years old. At the age of 18, he joined the British Army, and was based in North Africa when he heard of the execution of the leaders of the 1916 Rising, an event which inspired him to return home. During 1916 he was involved in intelligence with Sean Buckley in Bandon.

Donal McSweeney then outlined for me the dire situation created locally by the actions of the Crown forces and he says "… this Macroom group of Auxiliaries had to be tackled." During November 1920 Tom Barry began to train a group of Volunteers, and on 28th November at Kilmichael, an ambush was put in place from early morning. The men waited in position till five minutes past four in the afternoon when the Auxiliaries lorries were heard to approach.

Subsequent events on that fateful day were described to me in great detail by Meda Ryan and Donal McSweeney and Meda went on to tell me that she has spent years researching the events of the ambush itself and had spoken at length to some of the men who had participated on the day.

Much of the recording was made at the ambush site at Kilmichael on a cold and blustery November afternoon, and later we proceeded to Gougane Barra where Joe Creedon of Creedon's Hotel made us welcome and sang for the company that most evocative of songs "The Boys of Kilmichael."

Donal McSweeney (standing) with his aunt and cousins at Gortnafuinsion,
Ballyvourney c.1930 (courtesy of Donal McSweeney)

Jim Crowley, Clonakilty at Beál Na mBláth

CD No. 4

Time: 68.23

Publisher: Maurice O'Keeffe. ©

Michael Collins remains a towering figure in Irish history and his story has been told and retold. During 2004 I gathered some fascinating details about the man from five people who had stories to tell, namely Tim Crowley of Clonakilty, historians Ryle Dwyer and Meda Ryan, and two contemporaries of the great man, Patsy Holmes and Sean Clancy.

I met Tim Crowley at Woodfield, Collins' birthplace near Clonakilty. He told me that Michael was the youngest of eight children, born in 1890. At 15 years of age he began training as a post office clerk in Clonakilty, and in 1906 he went off to work in London. During my recording with Tim Crowley we travelled to the National School Collins attended at Lisavaird. The school dates from 1887 and Tim recalled for me the names of Michael's teachers, and spoke of the local blacksmith whose forge was situated across from the school – a place Michael visited regularly to listen to the blacksmith relate bloodcurdling stories of the Rebellion of 1798.

I next drove to Mallow where I spoke with Patsy Holmes, who at the grand old age of 102, has a vivid memory of shaking Collins' hand in Mallow the night before he was shot at Béal na mBláth

Col. Sean Clancy, aged 103 years welcomed me to Newtownpark Nursing Home in Dublin and spoke eloquently of his memories of meetings with Collins in Portabello Barracks.

Later, Meda Ryan accompanied me to Beál na mBláth, the "Mouth of the Flowers" where Collins died, and she spoke of the power struggle between Collins and de Valera prior to and during the Civil War. She pointed out the place where Collins breathed his last, and described in detail the events of that tragic day in August 1922.

I sat down with historian and author Ryle Dwyer one afternoon in Tralee and he provided for me a most interesting insight into the aftermath of the Beál na mBláth Ambush, and he spoke in great depth about the mood of the people in Ireland following the slaying of Michael Collins, who was considered invincible by so many people.

Michael Collins (Courtesy of Michael Finucane)

Paddy Gleeson, O'Callaghan's Mills, Co. Clare

CD No. 5

Time: 71.50

Publisher: Maurice O'Keeffe. ©

O'Callaghan's Mills was my destination one bright summer's evening in 2004, when a friend from Doolin, Gussie McMahon brought me to a lovely traditional cottage, the home of Paddy Gleeson who was born in 1904, in Scariff, Co. Clare.

We talked about his recollections of his early days, and he remembers how the mood of the people locally underwent a major change after the execution of the leaders of the 1916 Rising, with young people joining the Volunteer Movement as he did himself in 1917. The Movement began to engage in such activities as cattle driving, and on one occasion they approached the owners of the sawmills in Scariff and suggested that work should cease as Irish timber should not in future be exported to England. The Volunteers were met at the sawmills by Constable Cook and three men were arrested and charged. During the subsequent court case, which Paddy Gleeson attended, disruption by a crowd of republican sympathisers caused the case to be abandoned and as the prisoners were being marched down O'Connell Street in Ennis, a horse and cart was pulled in front of the military formation, allowing the men to escape through the melee. They were captured within the month and brought to Mountjoy prison in Dublin.

Paddy Gleeson recalled joining the Scariff Branch of the Boy Scout Brigade, formed by Countess Markeivicz, as all the local boys did in their early youth at that time.

My evening in O'Callaghan's Mills was well spent and I very much enjoyed sitting and talking with a man whose company I relished and whose recollections form such an important segment of the big picture that is our history.

The late Patsy Homes, Mallow, Co. Cork

CD No. 6A & 6B

Time: 49.59(A), 37.52(B)

Publisher: Maurice O'Keeffe. ©

Nazareth House in Mallow was the home of Patsy Holmes in his later years, and in May 2004 he celebrated his 102nd birthday there. Word came to me that here was a man who should be recorded, as his memory was very clear. That was enough for me, and I made arrangements to meet Patsy as soon as possible, and I am very glad that I did as he passed away the following year.

He was born in Whitechurch in 1902, and as a young man he found employment with a butcher in Mallow named Clancy, and during this time he drove cattle to and from fairs up and down the countryside. He recalls that many of his friends were involved with the Volunteer movement, and Patsy himself took part in a raid on the RIC Barracks in Fermoy where several guns were acquired, and he and others were subsequently arrested. They were brought to Spike Island and later put on a gun boat "The Heather" and taken to Ballykinlar near Downpatrick, where he was imprisoned for some time. He recalled a Maurice Donovan, a school teacher from Bantry, Co. Cork who was an excellent footballer, and on one occasion, a match was organised in prison between Munster and Leinster, and a total of 14 Kerry players turned out for Munster on that day.

A tunnel was built by the prisoners as a possible escape route but this collapsed on the very day that King George V visited Belfast.

Patsy sang for me several of the local rebel songs, which I had not heard before and which are virtually forgotten today. It was a real pleasure to meet Patsy Holmes and to listen enraptured to his stories and his songs.

William Geary in uniform of Garda Siochána

CD No. 7, 8, 9 and 10
Time: 60.30, 40.22, 77.33, 37.18
Publisher: Maurice O'Keeffe. ©

In June 2004, I was invited by the Irish American Historical Society in New York to come to the city to address them on my work involving the recording and archiving of local history and folklore. The Society also suggested that I record the memories of William Geary from Ballyagran, Co. Limerick who lived in New York. I was very pleased to be afforded the opportunity to meet this fascinating man, who had lived in three centuries – his young manhood lived in an Ireland in the grip of appalling turmoil.

I made my way to Bayside, New York and met William Geary, and his story held such fascination for me, I returned to record him a second time during that week. At that time he was 105 years old, and was to die peacefully less than six months later.

William began his life in Ballyagran. He was born in 1899, into a strong farming family. Following schooling locally he travelled to Caherciveen, Co. Kerry in 1918 to train as a wireless operator at the Atlantic Wireless School. Principal Maurice Fitzgerald awarded him a First Class Honour on his graduation. For a year he travelled the world as a ship's wireless operator, and then decided to return home, where he became involved in drilling the local Volunteers in Co. Limerick.

In May 1922 he joined the new Garda Siochána and served initially in Newbridge, Co Kildare. He was on duty in Dublin Castle along with many colleagues from Kildare on the day the British flag was lowered and "... the British marched out and we marched in."

Later he was on sentry duty by night at the Castle and remembers rifle fire "... all over the city." He was promoted to Acting Inspector and transferred to Clones, Co Monaghan, and later Templemore, Co Tipperary where two Gardai were dismissed for their failure to arrest an armed IRA man as the standard of discipline within the Garda force was extremely rigid.

On 10th June 1926 he was transferred to Kilrush, Co Clare as Superintendent. The IRA was active in the area, being involved in general harassment such as the burning of farmers' hay, though William contended that compensation was sometimes sought from the Government for hay which was otherwise set alight!

On 14th June 1928 he was summoned to the Old Ground Hotel in Ennis, in uniform, to meet Commissioner Eoin O'Duffy and Chief Superintendent of Detectives David Neligan. He was accused of accepting a £100 bribe from the IRA and was dismissed from the Garda Siochána on 25th June 1928.

He was devastated at this turn of events and returned home to Limerick. He made the decision to emigrate to New York, as he now had no prospects in Ireland, so shortly thereafter he booked his passage and sailed to New York, where he boarded for some time with his former nanny from Ballyagran, Miss Mary Ellen Keane.

He took various employments over the years and during the Second World War he joined the US Air Force. He married and reared a family, but always endeavoured to clear his name by writing to consecutive Ministers for Justice in Ireland. For all of seventy years he and his friends at home in Ireland never faltered in their efforts to get justice for him, and to have him fully exonerated.

Finally, in 2002 John O'Donoghue, Minister for Justice, restored his honour and travelled to New York to meet William Geary personally. After all the long and bitter years of battling for exoneration Mr Geary was elated and relieved and he lived out his final days in peace until his death in late 2004.

The Late William Geary, Limerick and New York

No. 8255.

UNITED KINGDOM OF GREAT BRITAIN AND IRELAND.

Certificate of Proficiency in Radiotelegraphy granted by the Postmaster General.

FIRST CLASS.

This is to certify that, under the provisions of the Radiotelegraph Convention, 1912, Mr. *William Geary* has been examined in Radiotelegraphy and has passed in—

(a) The working and adjustment of apparatus.

(b) Transmission and sound-reading at a speed of not less than 20 words a minute.

(c) Knowledge of the regulations applicable to the exchange of radiotelegraphic traffic.

The holder's practical knowledge of adjustment was tested on a *1½ kw. Marconi Standard* set of apparatus.*

His knowledge of other systems is shown below :—

— Not examined —

It is also certified hereby that the holder has made a declaration that he will preserve the secrecy of correspondence.

Signature of examining officer *[signature]*

The holder of this certificate is therefore authorized to operate wireless telegraph apparatus as a first class operator on board a British ship.

[signature] for Secretary, G.P.O., London.

23 August 1919. (Date).

Signature of holder *William Geary.*

Date of Birth *28 February, 1899.* Place of Birth *Cloonee, Co. Limerick.*

*It is not intended to limit the employment of the holder to a particular system, but merely to indicate the particular system in which he was tested for adjustment of apparatus.

This Certificate should be carefully preserved. In case of loss through avoidable causes, a duplicate will only be issued on payment of a fee of not less than 10s.

N.B.—This Certificate may be endorsed, or withdrawn, at the discretion of the Postmaster General, in case of misconduct or breach of the Regulations on the part of the holder. Unless so withdrawn, it will continue to be valid so long as the Regulations of the Radiotelegraph Convention concluded in London in 1912 remain in force.

K.515.

(23985) Wt. 28561—SP2317. 5000. 10/13. Sir J. C. & S. Gp. 153. F1152.

Certificate of Proficiency in Radiotelegraphy First Class Dated 23rd August 1919. Awarded to William Geary.

The Late Billy Mullins, Tralee, Co. Kerry

CD No. 11
Time: 76.31
Publisher: Maurice O'Keeffe. ©

This is a unique recording, previously unheard in public, and I feel very honoured to have gained access to it. It was given to me by Mr Eddie Barrett of Tralee, a grand nephew of Austin Stack. Mr Barrett made the recording with Billy Mullins of Tralee in November 1989, as he recognised the historical importance of the content and the quite advanced age of his interviewee.

The recording begins with Billy Mullins' recollections of Good Friday 1916, when, after Roger Casement's arrest and imprisonment in Tralee, a priest and a doctor were brought to the RIC Barracks to meet him. The priest was handed a message by the prisoner which was subsequently given to Paddy Cahill, an IRB member in Tralee. Billy Mullins was entrusted with delivery of the message to the military Council in Dublin where he met James Connolly who was in charge of the Citizen Army, along with other Council members.

The message, according to Billy Mullins read, "All the help that Germany could give was the boat load of arms." He recalled that the Council members showed no great interest in the contents of the message. He recognised one Council member as Sean McDermott who had previously come to Tralee to address the Volunteers at The Rink. On Easter Sunday 1916, word came from Dublin that the proposed Rising was cancelled and Billy Mullins maintained that this was a blessing in disguise as most of the Volunteers locally "… had more guts than guns" and would have been destroyed. Following the Rising in Dublin the Tralee Volunteers were arrested and transported initially to Richmond Prison in Dublin. Two months later Mullins was sent across the water to Wheatfield Prison in Yorkshire and later to Brixton Prison for a few weeks, finally being sent to Frongoch in North Wales, where be became friendly with Michael Collins and Cathal Brugha.

On his release he became Quartermaster of No.1 Brigade IRA in Kerry in 1920. He travelled regularly to Dublin where he met his contact in the Clarence Hotel. On one occasion he was brought to the junction at Townsend Street and Brunswick St. to the Dublin Metropolitan Barracks where Michael Collins had his office. He had bought money for guns from Kerry, and Collins counted the notes out in front of him - £700 in all. With Collins on that day was McNamara, an employee of Dublin Castle, who was bringing state secrets to Collins. "He was the real spy in the Castle" according to Billy Mullins. This is a reference to the book written by David Neligan "The Spy in the Castle."

I am very grateful to Mr Eddie Barrett for his permission to use this most fascinating and historic recording and also very thankful that he had the foresight to make the recording in November 1989.

The Late James Stack, Tralee, Co. Kerry and U.S.A.

CD No. 12

Time: 56.47

Publisher: Maurice O'Keeffe. ©

Early in April 2005, Mr Eddie Barrett of Tralee, a grandnephew of Austin Stack and James Stack, informed me that he had in his possession a hand-written account of events which occurred in Tralee during the years 1921 and 1922. This account under the title General Orders Book has not previously been publicly viewed and was written contemporaneously and in fascinating detail by James Stack, brother of Austin Stack.

Mr Barrett generously agreed to be interviewed in relation to his granduncle James, otherwise known as Jim, and he also read from some pages of the General Orders Book kept by his granduncle.

At a young age Jim Stack was employed in America and on hearing of the proposed Rising in 1916 in Ireland he stoked his way home to participate if possible, and he later returned to the U.S. Five years later in 1921 he came back to Tralee and was appointed quartermaster and Intelligence Officer with the IRA.

The entries in the General Orders Book make fascinating reading. The pages themselves are of a flimsy copy type, the originals having been torn out and given to messengers for delivery. The written words give a true and accurate account of day to day occurrences in and around Tralee during one of the most important periods in Irish history. Each entry is dated and signed by Jim Stack, until on 1st September 1922 he was arrested and imprisoned in The Curragh, where he later married Bess Mullins, sister of Billy Mullins of Tralee, Quartermaster No. 1 Brigade IRA.

I am sincerely grateful to Mr Eddie Barrett of Tralee for his cooperation in allowing me to use this previously unrecorded information and I am confident that it will be of great interest to historians. It is most gratifying to know that the information recorded is now in the public arena.

Eddie Barrett, Tralee, Co. Kerry.

33

To O/c Columns!
use to arrange for another
meeting. But Cahill would not
come. He said:—
5. Two Free Staters died from
wounds received in bombing
attack on Monday night
6. This officer two notions of
squashing Cahill to — be
charge in Kerry no 1.
His name is Finney a native
of Brosna. I knew him — met
him in Ballybunion last year
was in e. I. D. Dublin
We reamac very anxious
to speak Cahill. He both
(F.S.) of them as blasted
scoundrels. He is on to be very
friendly etc. He is calling
to-day very interesting, says
something interesting, says
Collins:—Cahill will split I. S.

32

Friday Aug 25th
1. Received yours last night
2. That night very quiet
3. Heard from H—— last
night find enclosed
You can see for yourself
House made in —— to
to receive staff.
4. H State of things in this house
last night for 3 hours had
a glorious time listening to
them. Bess pulled two of
He is a terrible liar said
there were hundreds of men
come to hunt on Wed last
and they were overcrowded
at Corhack contract this
with enclosed note from O.H.
He gave away about O.M.
Sunday n. ? of —— Brunehy
He is the guy that was doing
with probably e. He called

Pages from General Orders Book in the hand of James Stack, Intelligence Officer of the IRA.

RECOLLECTIONS OF 1916 AND ITS AFTERMATH

7. No doubt Collins was the only man to keep them together

8. Have not seen Molly Myles yet re - 3 grenades

9. Dispatches for different Butts. I am sending to Column 4. You made no mention of them in dispatch I presume Col 4 can have them sent to proper places.

10. Have instructed Cols 3.4.5 to block roads, to make them impassable. This will help in case of stunt in town

11. Saw Freemans Journal yesterday. Reports of several ambushes in Kerry no 1. Fennor Lynch + Owen O'Duffy were ambushed 3 times in one day in Kerry 1 area all narrow escapes no casualities.

36

While "shooting up" the town Wednesday night they put a bus into the priests house. Father Ferris's room got 2·303. Some joke Eh?

Drummond will be buried to-morrow. Have ordered wreath. Am sending mourning wreath. note paper & envelope get first to write Mrs Drummond or do it myself. Needless to say am not certain how his death came about everyone here still in doubt as to real facts.

Hope to meet you all at Fermoy on Sat or Sunday. Will let you know if any reinforcements arrive in meantime.

Lorries ... or 3 fine station every harbours two ... they watch roads from the night.

F.R.

---

17. Wires are working over-time. Cannot we have wires cut they seem to be able to do what they like with Telephone & Telegraph.

13 Description of bombing in Fermoy on Monday night & Two morning in Mich "Freeman" says there was a lorry load of Dublin guards waiting at Fermoy Barracks when Bombing started. They were men who to Leave ... and returning were wounded here and returning to Dublin. It also said that men inside Green Wall used rifles & revolvers.

14. No picket out that night. Car still calls to Brein & P.O. between 11. & 12 P.m.

15. No reinforcements as yet

16. Two reports from Mich Farmer Bill Herrington D.P. Conroher.

24

Thursday Aug 2[4]th
M. O'Connor
n capn

John Joe Sheehy told me
to write you and get you
to organize a few young
fellows around town for
Bombing etc what you can
do. Do you know where there
are any bombs planted in
town. If you get any information write it and send it
to me. Mark envelope E.B.
and leave it at Miss Kidney's
shop Castle St. Sign it
W.O.C. also let me know
how many young fellows
you can get for Bombing
Do this at once.
M. Stark

Do not do anything until
you tell me about it. Mes.

Ht. Q. Kerry No 1 I.R.18
Tralee Aug 19th 1922
To Oc Free State Army
Tralee

Information received to day
that Sergeant Ployden of
your army is to be buried
in the Republican Plot at
Rath Cemetery.
If this is correct I must
protest against it. This plot
was taken by the Republican
Army for soldiers of the Republic
and without the consent of
those who rented the plot
you or anyone else cannot
inter this the remains of any one
whatever they may be
Signed for and on behalf
of the Kerry No 1 Brigade
I.R.A.   J. M. Stark

Map of Kerry

CD No. 13

Time: 54.00

Publisher: Maurice O'Keeffe. ©

While collecting material for my local history recordings in the Irish Life and Lore series over the past eight years, I have been lucky enough to interview some people who witnessed this turbulent time in our history and I also interviewed five direct descendants of participants in the events in Kerry.

The Late Michael Scanlon, Ballymacdonnell, East Kerry

I called on Michael Scanlon from Ballymacdonnell, East Kerry in 2001. Michael was born in 1899. He recalled being in Tralee on Easter Monday morning 1916, having driven pigs from Ballymacdonnell to the fortnightly sale in Tralee. The word was out that Austin Stack had been arrested. Michael took a walk around town and saw a group of RIC men being fired on in The Mall. He told me that it was a "… hot spot to be in and you'd never know where the next bullet would come from." That violent incident stayed with him for the rest of his days until his death later in 2001.

Michael Finucane, Moyvane and Dublin

In the summer of 2004 I spoke to Michael Finucane, who was born in Moyvane in 1903, and now lives in Dublin. Michael's recollection is that the people of Kerry generally were unaware of any potential Rising, as the events to take place in Dublin were kept secret by the IRB. Few people in Tralee knew about Casement's imminent arrival at Banna Strand.

Michael told me "… the mood of the Kerry people at the time was that they didn't want any Rising, they were quite happy with the way life was, and there was no mention of the word 'republicanism'."

Ryle Dwyer, Tralee

I spoke to historian Ryle Dwyer about the events of that turbulent weekend. "Things went so wrong in Kerry; it took the British by surprise. The British were well aware of the plans for the Rising in advance. Because of the foul ups including the Ballykissane tragedy, the arrest of Casement and the taking of the *Aud,* Eoin McNeill had the rebellion called off and had inserted an advertisement in the newspapers calling off all manoeuvres for the weekend and the Irish leaders got together and rearranged the Rising for Easter Monday"

The Late Michael O'Leary, Castlegregory

Murt and Helen O'Leary of the
Maharees Islands

Austin Stack

In the early months of 2004 I met with Michael O'Leary, now sadly deceased, originally from Castlegregory, who was the son of Murt O'Leary of the Maharee Islands. In Holy Week 1916 Murt O'Leary was approached by three men from Tralee – Sheehy, Stack and Cahill – at Spillane's pub in Castlegregory (now Fitzgerald's). They told Murt that they were expecting just a handful of guns to come into Fenit on the *Aud* and asked him to pilot the boat into Fenit. The boat would come in to the north of Inishtooskert on Holy Saturday night. Security was so tight on that day that they said they would bring a lamp and a green jersey later though these items never arrived. If the *Aud* appeared during the day he would wear a green jersey and if by night he would flash the lamp. On Holy Thursday evening Murt saw the Aud coming up from the west. She seemed to be weighted down but wasn't flying a flag for a pilot to pilot her into Fenit, so he didn't take much notice of her. On Good Friday morning he saw a British patrol boat boarding her. The Captain of the *Aud* had false papers showing she was a Norwegian commercial ship, so the British went off feeling all was in order. A British destroyer came up from the west on Saturday morning and fired a shot across the bow of the ship and gave orders to follow her down to Queenstown harbour. All that happened before anyone in Tralee became aware of events. They read about it in the newspapers two days later. Michael O'Leary told me this story five weeks before he died as he was anxious to "… put the record straight."

Captain Monteith who accompanied Casement to Banna later revealed that the guns brought in by the *Aud* were completely out of date and that the ammunition was not compatible with the guns. The *Aud* was ordered to put into Cork harbour but was scuttled by the crew near Cobh, Co. Cork.

Owen Ring, Valentia

My journey then took me to Valentia Island to meet Diarmuid and Owen Ring, sons of Eugene and Tim Ring, locally known as the Ring Brothers. It was the Ring Brothers who alerted America and Germany to the Rising in Dublin before the British had fully realised that Dublin was up in arms. Diarmuid Ring told me that his father Tim worked for the Western Union in the cable office on Valentia with his brother Eugene. He was a member of the IRB and knew Cathal Brugha in London and idolised the man. When Brugha was shot, Tim lost heart and took no further part in militant affairs. Diarmuid Ring told me that his father Tim related to him how the message reached John Devoy, leader of the IRB in America. A girl in Kenmare filed the telegram and sent it to Tim Ring who forwarded the message. As they were aware of the work of the censors, the brothers had tested the safety of the system beforehand by sending a message to Newfoundland. Owen Ring, who lives in Renard, told me that in the weeks following the Rising, during an interview with a member of Clann na Gael in New York, it emerged that the message about the Rising came from a "… small fishing village in the West of Ireland." The Ring Brothers were arrested, Tim was sent to Frongoch and Eugene was incarcerated in Caherciveen barracks.

I asked Owen Ring what his father Eugene told him of the tragedy at Ballykissane Pier near Killorglin. He said that Volunteers travelling from Dublin, including local man Con Keating, a wireless expert, were driving towards Caherciveen during Holy Week 1916, to dismantle and relocate the naval wireless station for Republican use. A wrong turn at Killorglin had tragic results as the car drove off the pier in appalling weather conditions. Con Keating and two others were drowned. Local man Denis Daly survived because he was travelling in the second car.

The amazing thing about the Ring brothers' story is that they were acting for Padraig Pearse and the Dublin leaders of the Rising and were operating from the most heavily guarded centre of communications of the British Empire during the Great War of 1914-1918, as in 1914 a huge garrison of British troops was quartered in the island.

George Rice, Tralee

Back in Tralee, I had a very informative interview with George Rice of Ballyard, son of John Joe Rice, who arrived in Tralee from Kenmare in 1914 to work with the Great Southern Railways. He joined B Company, the Irish Volunteers under the direct command of Austin Stack. They lodged together in a boarding house in Upper Rock Street, now the premises of Barry's Supermarket. When Austin Stack was arrested on Easter weekend 1916, the local Volunteers paraded at the double through the town to show readiness for action. On Sunday, the Volunteers assembled under arms at the Rink, Basin View and including men from outlying areas they numbered about 1,000. Eoin McNeill's countermanding order arrived from Dublin and the Volunteers dispersed.

By amazing coincidence, George Rice told me that it was his aunt, Rosalie Rice from Kenmare Post Office, who filed the telegram for Tim Ring in Valentia Cable Station who was on duty the night of the Rising in Dublin. The coded message read – "Mother operated on successfully today." Signed Kathleen

"It was so important, at that time, to let the world know that Ireland had risen once again to defend her freedom," declared George Rice.

It was my privilege to interview and record, for posterity, the witnesses of the stirring events in Kerry, and their families, to whom I owe a great debt of gratitude for their kindness and cooperation.

The Rice Family, Kenmare c. 1898
On the extreme left is Rosalie Rice, who filed the telegram from Kenmare Post Office for
Tim Ring in Valentia Cable Station to alert America and the world to the Rising of 1916

Pictured above, Robert Monteith (second from left, with moustache) Private Daniel Bailey (third from left) and Roger Casement (fifth from left) on board the submarine U-20

John Scannell, Annascaul, Co. Kerry

CD No. 14

Time: 36.00

Publisher: Maurice O'Keeffe. ©

John Scannell was born in September 1903 and he now resides in Ocean View Nursing Home in Camp, Tralee where I visited him in early 2001. He grew up in Cromdubh in Annascaul in what was to become a safe house for the Volunteers in the years leading up to the Civil War.

John Scannell recalled for me his clear memories of the Lispole Ambush of March 1921. It had been known that every Sunday the Black and Tans would travel on patrol from Dingle towards Camp, and would "... fire a few shots" in the village. One Saturday evening the Volunteers gathered in the old school with the intention of ambushing the Tans on the Sunday. John Scannell told me that the British had 'information' so they did not appear until the following Wednesday, when they set up a machine gun and began firing at the school roof. The Volunteers escaped into a nearby glen but four of their members were wounded, three men fatally. John also recalls the wounding of Tom Ashe of Lispole, cousin of the patriot Thomas Ashe of Kinard, who was carried to a local house where he died later the same night.

The Civil War which followed was "... much worse" and John told me that on one occasion the Company Captain of the Volunteers stood in the sloping street in Annascaul and instructed the people of the village as follows: ... those in favour of the Treaty "come up" and those against "stay below". About 100 men moved up and only two stayed below, according to John.

I was reluctant to take my leave of John Scannell, one of nature's gentlemen and a fount of valuable information on stormy days in our history.

Archdeacon Rowland Blennerhassett, Fenit, Co. Kerry

CD No. 15

Time: 75.14

Publisher: Maurice O'Keeffe. ©

I had the pleasure of making the acquaintance of Archdeacon Blennerhassett some years ago, and I have always admired his great knowledge of local history, and in particular the history of Tralee town in the early part of the 20th century.

Rowland Blennerhassett was born in Caherina, Tralee in 1909, and his father George was Secretary of McCowan's Shamrock Mills in the town. In the course of his work George Blennerhasset travelled around the countryside on a sidecar and on one occasion in 1920 Rowland and his brother accompanied their father to Newcastlewest, Co Limerick. Towards evening, Mr Blennerhassett became aware of some trouble in the area so he left hurriedly with his sons and stayed overnight in Abbeyfeale. While crossing the mountain road near Knocknagoshel the following morning, they were approached by a man on horseback and instructed to bring a passenger to Tralee. Shortly afterwards a man appeared carrying explosives and a revolver. The Blennerhassett family had no option but to bring him to Tralee, and the following day, Rowland Blennerhassett clearly recalls spotting their passenger of the previous morning walking down Castle Street in Tralee dressed in priest's clothing.

During the occupation of Tralee, the Black and Tans imposed a curfew and one evening he and his father were fired on for breaking the curfew and they had to make a dash for home. Minutes later a young man, attempting desperately to take cover, cleared the Blennerhassett's garden wall and hid in a shed on the property, but he was discovered by the British soldiers and dragged away and was later shot.

On the 15th April 1921 Major John McKinnon of the Auxiliaries was shot at the old golf course in Tralee and on the following days the Auxiliaries undertook an orgy of destruction and the town was closed down for the greater part of a week, a fact clearly recalled by Archdeacon Blennerhassett.

During 1921/1922 there was a certain animosity felt towards the Protestant residents of Tralee and threatening letters were received but fortunately not by the Blennerhassett family as Mr George Blennerhassett "…played both sides" as his son recalls.

I spoke to the Archdeacon in his 96th year at his Fenit home and it was a real pleasure for me to listen to his recollections of the people and events which shaped his early youth in Kerry.

Knocknagoshel 1923
Civilian is searched by Free State soldiers

Rowland Blennerhassett,,
Caherina Villa, Tralee. c.1920

Margaret Kennedy Doughan, Templemore, Co. Tipperary

CD No. 16

Time: 46.25

Publisher: Maurice O'Keeffe. ©

In October 2003 I was invited to attend the Roscrea Conference at Mount St Josephs to launch the Irish Life and Lore collection of recordings in the Midlands. The conference organiser George Cunningham, suggested I make contact with Margaret Doughan of Templemore and endeavour to record her vivid memories of times past in Tipperary and Waterford.

Born in 1915 in Waterford city she remembers as a small child watching through the window of her home as the British soldiers on drill manoeuvres on horseback, followed by a brass band, paraded around the streets, an event which occurred three times a week.

In the early 1920s the family moved to Puckane in Co Tipperary, and Margaret recalled that one evening some unwelcome visitors arrived at a relative's house, where her father was taking shelter from a downpour. He was relaxing in bed while his clothes were drying before the fire when an Auxiliaries lorry pulled up outside, and the soldiers trampled through the house. They intended to take her father hostage, but a local RIC man, who happened to be passing, entered the house and succeeded in persuading the Auxiliaries that he had no involvement in the Movement. A few days later, in a nearby house, two O'Brien men were taken away by the Auxiliaries and were later shot.

Margaret Kennedy's aunt, Nora Kennedy, had an interesting story to tell, and Margaret recounted it for me. Nora Kennedy boarded with Nellie Keating, an aunt of Michael Collins, in Drumcondra, Dublin. Nellie was a member of Cumann na mBan. The night before Collins travelled on his fateful journey to Cork in August 1922, he came to the house in Drumcondra at 11 o'clock, to stay overnight. His aunt Nellie made valiant efforts to dissuade him from travelling south, but when his hat and coat were missing from the hallway in the morning, Nora Kennedy knew that Nellie had been unsuccessful and that Michael Collins had left for Cork.

Before I left, Margaret Doughan entrusted to me a fascinating collection of letters, hand-written by Dr John O'Donovan, the great Celtic scholar, in the 1840s and this collection of very valuable historical letters is now housed in the Royal Irish Academy, which acquired the collection in early 2004.

Magaret Kennedy Doughan, as a young girl with her parents and family. c. 1925.

The late Nora Costello Humphreys, Newport, Co. Tipperary

CD No. 17A & 17B

Time: 71.42(A), 45.04(B)

Publisher: Maurice O'Keeffe. ©

I was introduced to Nora Humphreys in October 2004 in Newport, Co Tipperary where she lived, and we spoke at length about her days in Clonbeg, Thurles, where she was born in 1917. She came from a family of seven children and was looked after by a nanny named Nell Devaney, who came to the family at the young age of 14 years.

In June 1919, Nell decided to spend her day off at Thurles Races, and on her return home, she was alight with of excitement about the events of the day. The local District Inspector of Police, Michael Hunt had been shot in the Square in the town. Inspector Hunt was a most unpopular individual, and he met his fate that day at the hands of two local boys, Sean Dunne and Jim Stapleton, both of whom were related to Nora's mother.

"Big Jim" Stapleton and Sean Dunne had had the Inspector under observation since leaving the racetrack and on reaching the Square, Stapleton drew his revolver and shot him at close range. Immediately Canon Ryan ran from across the Square to administer the Last Rites. Stapleton and Dunne ran from the scene, up Post Office Lane and scaled an eight foot wall to make their escape. They crossed the river three times that night as they made their way to Ryan Lacken's house at Knockfune. Matt Larkin was sent for and he arrived from Clonacke with a horse and trap. He brought the two boys to Killaloe, where they were met by friends who looked after them. Sean Dunne was very ill with pneumonia and needed constant care. He was later to become a Captain in the Irish Army, and died at the tragically young age of 27 years.

Nora spoke eloquently of life in rural Tipperary in her young days and had interesting things to say about the mood of the ordinary people in the countryside in the early part of the 20th century.

She sang for me that evocative old song "The Three Flowers" recalling three great men who shaped our history, and who are remembered with great pride in this old ballad. Sadly Nora Humphreys passed away in May 2005.

Dan Keating, Ballygamboon, Castlemaine, Co. Kerry

CD No. 18

Time: 68.14

Publisher: Maurice O'Keeffe. ©

I have had the pleasure of knowing Dan Keating for many years and because I had recorded his recollections in the past, I was aware that he was a mine of information on events in this country during the early days of the 20th century.

I travelled to Dan's home in March 2005 and immediately we settled ourselves, it became obvious that he was anxious to return in memory to the turbulent days of his early youth in rural Kerry.

Dan was born in January 1902 and at the age of 14 years, he remembers hearing about a large contingent of Volunteers which had gathered at The Rink in Tralee on Easter Sunday 1916. One of the organisers was Paddy Cahill, who was later to be involved in the Lispole Ambush.

In 1921 Dan Keating joined the IRA Boherbee B Company. He named for me the different IRA divisions in Tralee and their respective leaders. He spoke about the several British Regiments occupying the Barracks in the town – The Scottish Borderers, the Essex Regiment and the Lancashire Regiment – "The Lancs" and he maintained that "The Lancs" treated the people more humanely than some of their counterparts.

Dan was involved in the Castlemaine Ambush in June 1921 where five RIC men were killed and several others wounded and spoke of his memories of that day. The previous April Denny O'Loughlin had been shot by the IRA in Knightley's Bar in Lower Bridge Street, Tralee, and Dan says that he and Jimmy "Nuts" O'Connor and Percy Hanafin were 'fingered' for this and went on the run. They spent a lot of their time in safe houses around Firies where there was always a welcome for them.

While famed Kerry footballer, John Joe Sheehy of Tralee was still on the run in 1924, his friend from North Kerry, Con Brosnan, a Free State Army Officer, went to Dublin to plead with Headquarters to allow him a week without capture before and after the All-Ireland Final. The Kerry team which went on to win the Final that year was captained by one John Joe Sheehy.

Dan Keating, Castlemaine, Co. Kerry and Nollaig O Gadhra, Galway

CD No. 19A & 19B

Time: 76.82(A), 38.50(B)

Publisher: Maurice O'Keeffe. ©

Nollaig O Gadhra is a well known historian, author and broadcaster and on hearing that I was working on recording "Recollections of 1916 and its Aftermath" he asked to be introduced to Dan Keating of Ballygamboon, of whom he had heard on many occasions. On Good Friday 2005 we sat down in Dan Keating's kitchen and began our work.

Nollaig outlined for Dan his own Kerry connections. His mother Hannah Flynn came from 'over the fields' in Firies and his uncle Jim Flynn was in 'the movement' with Tom McEllistrum.

It was decided that Nollaig O Gadhra would put the questions on this occasion so I sat back with my recorder to listen to a fascinating account of a fascinating life.

Nollaig began by enquiring about Dan's earliest recollections of British recruitment in Tralee during the Great War, the Fenian movement in Tralee, the prevailing mood in Kerry during Easter 1916, the round up of Volunteers after The Rising and the complete reversal of attitudes locally following the execution of the leaders in Dublin. There was talk of proposed enforced conscription by the British resulting in many young men joining the Volunteers. The death of Thomas Ashe from Kinard, Lispole also proved a major catalyst for many people who joined the movement.

There was discussion of the ambushes of the Auxiliaries and Black and Tans in Kerry, the Sinn Féin courts, which Dan maintained were very successful, and he recalled a humorous incident in Mountjoy prison where he was incarcerated one Ash Wednesday morning.

As we prepared to leave Ballygamboon that Good Friday, I was filled with admiration for this extraordinary man whom God has spared to enjoy a long and fruitful life and who is now in his 103rd year.

CD No. 20

Time: 56.57

Publisher: Maurice O'Keeffe. ©

During the summer of 2004 Michael Finucane was on holiday in Killarney with his family so I travelled there to meet him.

Michael was born in Newtownsandes, later known as Moyvane, in May 1903. He was taught in National School by John B. Keane's father and Bryan McMahon's father – a literary education indeed.

News of the Rising in Dublin on Easter Monday 1916 took some time to trickle through to Newtownsandes. Not many people locally were too interested in Republican matters, and felt that the Rising was a somewhat similar event to that organised by Jim Larkin in 1913.

Later in life Michael worked in the Civil Service with a man named Paddy Boland who had been imprisoned in Germany during the Great War. He recalled an occasion when Roger Casement visited the prison camp in an attempt to get the Irish inmates interested in a potential Rising at home and he said that not one prisoner was prepared to become involved with him, as most people were loyalist, on Home Rule terms, and had been fighting with the British during the war.

After the Rising the mood of the people in Ireland swung towards the Volunteers and Michael's elder brother, Paddy began 'training' in a local field with his friends in an atmosphere more reminiscent of a football match.

During June 1921, there was an air of quiet around the countryside but Michael recalls that during that month, as he was retuning from holidays in Clare by boat to Tarbert, he was met in the village by a British soldier who demanded that his suitcase be opened, whereupon he searched carefully among the contents with his bayonet before allowing Michael to proceed.

He recalled that directly before the Black and Tans left Ireland he was walking through Listowel with IRA man Con Brosnan when they spotted twelve Tans standing outside the Barracks in the town. He remembers Con crossing the road and introducing himself. The men were stupefied, saying that they had been hunting for him for the previous two years without success.

During his years in the Civil Service, Michael worked with many people who had been involved with the fight for freedom, and knew David Neligan, who played a prominent part in the events of the Civil War.

My day in Killarney with Michael Finucane was very well spent, and I was very glad to have had an opportunity to listen to his fine reminiscences and recollections.

Michael Finucane and Kathleen Deasy c. 1930's

North Kerry Flying Column photographed at Coolard outside Listowel: front row left to right: Patrick J. McElligott, Denis Quille, James Sugrue, Brian O'Grady; second row: Martin Quille, Christopher Broader, Cornelius Brosnan, Timothy O'Sullivan; back row: Daniel O'Grady, Miss Mary Aherne, and Sean Coughlan

Des and Pam Cooke, Tralee, Co. Kerry

CD No. 21

Time: 42.00

Publisher: Maurice O'Keeffe. ©

One cold day in October 2004, I fell into conversation on the street in Tralee with Pam Cooke, who, with her husband Des is retired and living in the town. I was fascinated to hear that they had in their possession a very historic letter dated 16th May 1920, which had been written locally.

Pam Cooke invited me to visit their home, and shortly afterwards, we sat around their bright fire one evening and Des began by telling me about his father's first visit to Tralee from his home in Reading in England in 1909. Charles Cooke drove to Tralee in a Model T Ford, to begin work as a chauffeur for the Crosby family of Ballyheigue Castle. Having worked with the family for some years he left their employment in 1916 to begin his own hackney business with his brother-in-law Harry Flower, who had arrived from Reading in 1908.

After Charles Cooke married, he arrived in the Gresham Hotel in Dublin to begin his honeymoon on Easter Saturday 1916, and on the Monday morning he left the hotel to take a walk down O'Connell Street. When he failed to return for many hours his bride began to worry as she listened to the sustained gunfire outside the windows of the hotel. Charles eventually returned, having been caught up in the fighting on O'Connell Street and been unable to return for several hours. On leaving the city shortly afterwards the couple had to obtain a permit to return home to Kerry.

The hackney business flourished in Tralee during the following years until, on 16th May 1920, threatening letters arrived at the homes of Charles Cooke, Harry Flower and Frank Cooke, a brother of Charles who had come to live in Tralee. Harry Flower and his wife Min and Frank Cooke feared for their lives and decided to leave, but Charles Cooke made a decision to 'stand up to them' and he continued to drive his hackney as before. He had a family to rear and a business to run, and bravely faced each day and what it would bring.

He lived out his life in safety, but it was never possible to forget the stark words written in the letter sent to him in May 1920.

"Take notice that if your car is caught running in town or country it will be smashed and you will be shot. By order of Vertias" (sic)

On the reverse side is a crude drawing of a coffin bearing the words "C Cooke shot RIP" and underneath it is drawn a rifle with the words "This is your death warrant driving after this notice."

Charles Cooke at the wheel of his hackney car in 1916
(Courtesy of Des Cooke)

TAKE NOTICE THAT IF
YOUR CAR IS CAUGHT RUNNING IN
TOWN OR COUNTRY iT WILL
BE SMASHED AND YOU WILL
SHOT. BY ORDER VERTIAS.

THIS IS YOUR DEATH WARRANT
DRIVING / AFTER THIS NOTICE.

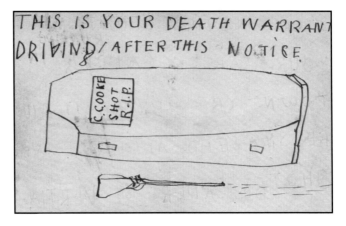

Upper Castle Street, Tralee. Charles Cooke's hackney business was run from the premises beside the car on the left.
(Courtesy of James Kelliher)

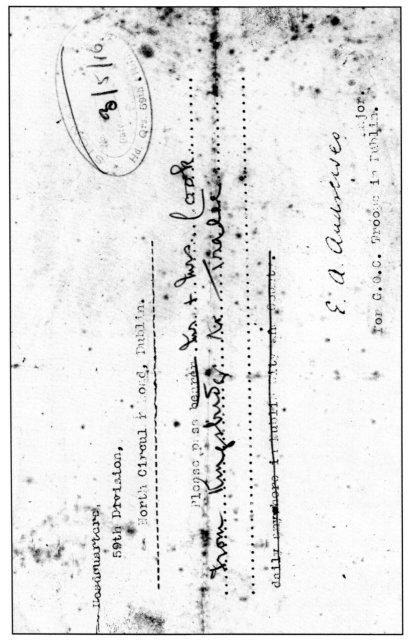

Headquarters,

59th Division,

— North Circular Road, Dublin.

Please pass bearer Mr. + Mrs. Cook ....
from Kingsbridge to ....Tralee.............
....
daily powsheer from Dublin City on foot.

E. A. Andrews

for G.O.C. Troops in Dublin. ....jor.

Official permit dated 5th May 1916 allowing Mr & Mrs Cooke to travel from Kingsbridge, Dublin to Tralee.

Eileen Sprague, Dublin and Killarney, Co. Kerry

CD No. 22

Time: 61.00

Publisher: Maurice O'Keeffe. ©

I was first introduced to Eileen Sprague in Killarney during the autumn of 2000 and I recorded her recollections at that time, and as she reminisced it became obvious to me that her memory was excellent with regard to historical detail of events in the early days of the 20th century in Dublin city.

Shortly afterwards I paid a return visit to Eileen in her home in Killarney and she began by telling me that she was born in 1907 in Belfast and at the age of one, she was sent to live with her grandmother at No. 9, Charles Street, Dublin.

When she was thirteen, she watched a large crowd gather outside Mountjoy Jail on the eve of Kevin Barry's execution on All Saints Day in November 1920. People were holding lighted candles and reciting The Rosary right through the hours of darkness. Kevin Barry's mother was amongst the crowd outside the jail and she was invited inside but she refused and remained with the crowd, in a very distressed state. The people continued to pray that Barry be shot as a patriot rather than being hung, as he had been arrested in uniform. Eileen's grandmother told her that she was acquainted with the woman who approached the British officer and told him that Kevin Barry was hiding under a lorry, after the gun battle in which he was involved. This information led to his arrest and death in Mountjoy.

Later that same month, on Bloody Sunday, Eileen's grandmother with whom she lived, saw a young man, gravely wounded, come over the wall at Croke Park and stagger, bleeding profusely, up Emmet Street and take refuge in a small Protestant church in Charles Street, leaving a trail of blood in his wake. Eileen's grandmother and a friend went to his assistance, but the Black and Tans, having followed the trail of blood, dragged the wounded man out and threw him onto their lorry. Eileen's grandmother became very agitated and called out to the Tans "You have mothers too don't you?"

We later went on to talk of Matt Talbot, of Eileen's schooldays in Dublin and of life in the capital city in those days.

My time with Eileen Sprague was a rare joy and her clear recollections of other days and their tragic events brought the past vividly to life for me.

Irish Rebellion, May, 1916.
A group of Officers, with the captured rebel flag.

Paddy Hurley, Athea, West Limerick

CD No. 23

Time: 58.05

Publisher: Maurice O'Keeffe. ©

As I was working in West Limerick collecting folklore and local history, I met with Paddy Hurley, a retired publican in Athea, and a man in his 91st year. We sat down to talk in the comfortable back kitchen in his home, and my questions began.

Paddy was born in Athea village and attended the local thatched school. He named for me all the families and businesses in the village of his youth, and went on to sing a local ballad, now rarely if ever heard.

As a young boy, he remembers the lorries of the Black and Tans passing through the village on their patrols from Listowel to Limerick. They invariably stopped at the local public houses, including his father's premises and demanded bottles of whiskey and brandy, which they would drink and then leave without any mention of payment.

One day when his older sister Margaret was twelve years old the Tans were drinking in the family public house. One of their number spotted her playing with her pet dog. On enquiring as to the dog's name, she told him he was called 'Rebel'. To her utter consternation he drew his revolver and shot the dog, an event which left an enduring effect on the young girl for the rest of her days.

Time went by and an ambush of the Black and Tans was set up in Brosna during which an IRA man was wounded and he was brought to Maurice Ahern's house to be cared for. At this time a nurse by the name of Molly White had returned from England where she had worked during the Great War period. There was great excitement locally when she arrived home having been driven by hackney all the way from Dublin, an unheard of occurrence in those days. She took on the task of nursing the IRA man in secret and they later fell in love, married and settled down.

Paddy Hurley finished by recalling a great patriot, local man Con Colbert, his siblings and his home place, and before I left his home, he sang for me the old refrain "Rose of Killarney" a sweet and nostalgic air, sung on that occasion by a man who loved and lived every word of the old song.

ATHEA (CO. LIMERICK) NATIONAL VOLUNTEERS AND RED CROSS NURSING STAFF

This photo appeared in the "Cork Weekly Examiner and Weekly Pictorial Supplement" on August 8th, 1914.

Hannah Crowley O'Connor, Ballyduff, Co. Kerry

CD No. 24

Time: 56.23

Publisher: Maurice O'Keeffe. ©

In early 2004, it was suggested to me that I should make contact with Hannah Crowley O'Connor, as it was known locally that I was recording for Radio Kerry, and for archiving, some elderly people who had truly fascinating information to relate.

During the course of my recording with Hannah, who was born in 1911, I enquired about her memories of the Black and Tans in Kerry. She remembered, at the age of 10, while returning home from school with her friends, they would look forward to hearing the Tans' lorries approach as the men would throw apples to the children from the lorries.

Her father, James Crowley, who had played on the winning Kerry hurling team of 1891, was on one occasion, being searched by the Black and Tans, as they had heard that he had made a derogatory remark about them. Hannah recalled the Tans arriving at their home and shouting twice "James Crowley, are you inside now?" and having received no response, searched the house in vain.

She remembered the occasion of a shooting of a young man called John Houlihan by the British in the village of Ballyduff and she told me that his distraught mother was brought out to witness the awful event.

In the summer months of 2004 I met Jack Farmer, who was born into a small farm near Headford, outside Killarney in 1912. We sat around a turf fire and Jack recalled the old farming traditions of his youth. He spoke of being hired out at thirteen years of

Jack Farmer, Killarney, Co. Kerry

age as a farm labourer. He lifted his fine voice to sing the well known ballad about the Headford Ambush and he told me that he recalled, at the age of nine, a group of IRA men busy in a wood at the bottom of the farm, preparing for a proposed ambush. This plan was later changed, and the famous Headford Ambush of March 1921 took place in its stead. He heard every shot fired on that long day, and he was in such dread he hid under the kitchen table. He recalled seeing IRA men passing through the fields to the ambush site on the previous day.

His family home was raided by the Black and Tans on the evening following the ambush, and everything was "pulled around" and the family "scared to death" during those long hours.

Dan "Bán" O'Shea, Caherciveen, Co. Kerry

I made my way to Caherciveen in May 2004 to meet Dan "Bán" O'Shea of whom I had heard a great deal. We met in the kitchen of his premises, a well-known public house which closed a few years ago. Dan "Bán" is now 90 years of age.

One of his clearest memories is of a Black and Tan called Allen, who slipped and injured himself having climbed onto a shed on the family premises. He threatened the family that the house would be burnt as a result of his injury, an unfounded threat which caused the family untold worry.

He remembers, as a very young child, being placed in the front seat of a truck with two Volunteers, James O'Connor and "Curley" Shannon, as a form of cover for them as the left Caherciveen to bring fish from his father's business to the Volunteers in Dublin.

The late Mike Christopher O'Shea, Caherciveen, Co. Kerry

In 2003 I talked to Mike Christopher O'Shea, also of Caherciveen who has sadly since died. I was in Caherciveen one day collecting folklore, and Mike was sitting on his windowsill at his premises in the Main Street of the town, taking the air. I stopped to chat and it was soon apparent that here was a man with stories to tell. He graciously invited me inside, where he showed me a collection of old Republican photographs and also some of early Kerry GAA teams.

Mike Christopher O'Shea was born in 1917 and he remembered his father telling him of an occasion when Miah O'Connell, father of the famous Valentia Island footballer Mick O'Connell, came to Caherciveen from Beginish Island. As the Angelus bell began to ring, he removed his cap and knelt down on one knee in the street to pray the Angelus. He was approached by two members of the Black and Tans, Copper and Allen, and ordered to say "To hell with the Pope". Mr O'Connell refused to comply with this demand, and at this point, Mike O'Shea's father attempted to intervene and was told in no uncertain terms to move away. The Tans then mercilessly beat Miah O'Connell with their rifle butts, and when they had finished they walked calmly away. Mike recalled an apprentice tailor by the name of Walsh who worked with Mike's father. He came from Valentia and was a member of the Volunteers. He and his comrades had guns and ammunition hidden in his employer's house and Mike told me that the arms were brought to another safe house on the very night before the O'Shea house was raided by the Black and Tans.

Mike's father and two of his friends Jack and Sean Connor, decided on one bright day to go beagling at Foilmore and they noticed just as they were leaving town that they were being followed by six Auxiliaries. To their amusement, they had no trouble avoiding the Auxiliaries all day, due to their local knowledge of the countryside until, at dusk, they decided they'd be safer at home in Caherciveen.

Mike O'Shea laughed as he told me this story, and he then proudly recited for me a poem written by himself and dedicated to his great hero Michael Collins.

The late Roy Mooney, The Doon, Co Offaly

CD No. 25
Time: 60.00
Publisher: Maurice O'Keeffe. ©

One spring evening in 2004 I made my way to The Doon, Co. Offaly, near Clonmacnoise to make my acquaintance with Roy Mooney. As I drove up the long avenue, and the lovely Georgian home of the Mooney family came into view, I had the feeling that this journey of mine would be very fruitful. Roy himself came to the door as I arrived unannounced, and bade me welcome. He became quite animated and very interested once I explained the purpose of my visit.

At that time, Roy was ninety years old, and once we were seated, I began by asking him about his family background and about his earliest memories. As a very young boy he had a most frightening experience, clearly and explicitly recalled for me that evening at his home.

During the occupation by the Black and Tans the soldiers would travel each day on patrol from Athlone to Birr, and generally, they were the worse for wear if not drunk, firing at random at the trees and ditches along the way. One day the Republicans knocked a tree across the road and dug a trench at Ballynahown, very close to the Mooney home. The Tans arrived on the scene, used planks of wood to cross the trench, and sped on, only to ram the lorry into the fallen tree. Panic ensued, with the soldiers firing indiscriminately. Roy clearly recalls the clamour of the guns and the bullets whizzing off the front of his house. Shortly thereafter, a further lorry load of Tans arrived on the scene, and such was the pandemonium that two of their number were shot and wounded by their colleagues in the first lorry. Eventually they retreated and all was quiet once again.

That night a group of Republicans commandeered the house and demanded lodgings for the night, and Roy recalled being told that he had to give up his bed. A false message was relayed from the village that the Tans were approaching so the Republicans fled across the fields.

A story from an earlier era was told to me by Roy. It concerned a visit to the house by Robert Emmet after the Rebellion of 1803 in Dublin. One evening, he came to the back door, dishevelled and exhausted, and asked to see the master. The servants brought him in and gave him a good meal, on their master's instructions, as he appeared to be in very bad shape. Roy's great grandfather, who was the master of the house at that time always afterwards remarked on the excellent table manners and general politeness of the man, who thanked him profusely for his hospitality before departing.

I continued to talk to Roy Mooney for several hours, and later returned, when I recorded him a second time, along with his gracious wife Kitty, whose memories, like those of her husband, make fascinating listening. Sadly I was later to hear that Roy Mooney had died not long after the second recording was made.

Lily Ryle, Farmers Bridge, Tralee, Co. Kerry

Farmers Bridge, outside Tralee was my destination one day in August 2004, and there I visited Lily Ryle at her stone cottage where she greeted me warmly and shook my hand over the half-door, and a fine firm grip she has.

Lily Ryle was born in 1906 in Caherlaheen, a short distance away and her maiden name was Kelliher. As a child she remembers walking the mile and a half to school, and being afraid of meeting the lorries of the Auxiliaries "with the Cowboy hats". She told me of two notorious Black and Tans who were stationed in Tralee, "Big Paddy" and "The Jew" who would terrorise the population of Farmers Bridge each night as they had a "dead set" against the people there.

Lily has a clear recollection of seeing the coffins of the victims of the Ballyseedy massacre of March 1923. The coffins had been placed outside the wall of Tralee Barracks and the distraught relatives were attempting to identify the remains. This stark and distressing sight has stayed firmly in Lily's memory to this day.

Br. Charles Quinn, Iona College, New York

During my trip to New York, in June 2004 to address the Irish American Historical Society, I was advised to seek out Brother Charles Quinn, past Dean and Vice President of Iona College, New Rochelle. I spoke to Br. Quinn by telephone initially and he was quite prepared to share his recollections and memories, both of his American childhood and of his subsequent years in Co. Clare prior to his return to the U.S. as a Christian Brother.

I arranged to meet him at Iona College and I subsequently recorded many hours of fascinating material with this most interesting man. He was born in Boston in 1913 and one of his earliest memories is of sitting on his father's shoulders watching Eamon de Valera speak on one of his visits to the United States. At the age of 10 years, Charles came to live in Ennistymon, Co Clare, with his family. His grandfather had died and his father inherited the family farm. Charles attended school in Ennistymon where a popular game played by the students was the Republicans versus the Free Staters. He recalled that the bitterness and animosity engendered by the Civil War was still very much in evidence, and it was years before the negative feelings were to dissipate somewhat, when the economic war diverted peoples' minds from the horror of those cruel days.

Charles' father did not take sides in the Civil War but he did support the Irish Societies while living in America prior to returning home to Co. Clare.

We went on to speak of Charles' memories of the West Clare Railway, of emigration to Boston and New York in later years and of his own fascinating life and times.

Kitty Duggan Weir, Abbeydorney, Co. Kerry

Kitty Duggan Weir is a retired nurse who lives in Abbeydorney, near Tralee, and she recently invited me to her home to view some historical photographs which she had inherited from her sister many years ago.

When I arrived at Kitty's home and looked at the album of photographs, I enquired of her if she would be willing to have the fascinating story behind the photographs recorded, and she was very happy to do so.

Kitty's sister also trained as a nurse, and she looked after an elderly lady in Dublin who gave her the album of photographs. The lady was born in Ballybunion, Co. Kerry and was acquainted with Kitty's family, the Duggans.

Her name was Eily O'Flaherty, whose father was Morgan O'Flaherty, a schoolteacher in Ballybunion and her mother was Mary Pierce from Ballyduff. Morgan O'Flaherty died at a young age, leaving a family of four children, and Eily and her sister Anne left home in their late teens, to travel to Dublin and begin nurse training. They both joined Cumann na mBan, and Eily became involved with delivering arms to Austin Stack in Kerry. She would travel by train and would be met by a messenger from Tralee at Kilmorna Station.

On one occasion she was followed by the military from the station to her mother's house in Ballybunion, and the house was searched but nothing was found as Eily had hidden the arms on the bottom leaf of an extension dining table.

On another occasion she knew she was being followed, so she hid the cache of arms in the altar of the Catholic church in Ballybunion, until the parish priest discovered this and was furious with the young girl.

Looking through the photograph album, Kitty Weir pointed out a photograph of Eily O'Flaherty with a comrade in arms, a photograph of members of the North Kerry Flying Column, the Clashmealcon Caves as a backdrop to Republican training, the original monument at Clashmealcon and many others.

Kitty Weir's mother had strong Republican sympathies, and would talk for hours with Eily O'Flaherty while on her visits home to Ballybunion, and when Eily was in her last days on this earth she entrusted the album of historic photographs to the Duggan family knowing that they and her remarkable life story would be preserved and honoured.

Rory Sweeney, Ballybunion, Co. Kerry

In April 2005, I was preparing a documentary for radio on rural creameries in Kerry and I interviewed Rory Sweeney, who is in his 86th year and living in Ballybunion. As we spoke, he recalled that his father, William T. Sweeney had been the proprietor of a large creamery at Shannonvale, Ballyduff, he recalled the tragic days of the occupation by the Black and Tan Forces in the 1920s and told me that his father's creamery was burnt along with part of the dwelling house, and that his father went on the run with a price of £1,000 on his head.

I was fascinated by this information and a few weeks later I returned to Ballybunion to

The Late Bill Sweeney, Ballyduff, Co. Kerry 1915

sit and talk with Rory once again. His father's business encompassed a large creamery, which had been previously amalgamated with two smaller local creameries, a grocery shop and a thriving fish business. The arrival of the Black and Tans created chaos in the locality and after the burning of the creamery, his father went on the run. A price of £1,000 was put on his head as it was known that he was an excellent organiser of men, and a very influential character. "He knew the pulse of the people."

In later years he was reluctant to speak of those volatile times but he would regularly speak at meetings and from the back of his truck in the Republican cause prior to elections.

Rory recalled a dramatic story told to him by his mother Nell. During the period of the Black and Tan occupation, while her husband was on the run, the forces came to the house one day and demanded that all the presses and drawers in the house be opened for their inspection. Nell was horrified as she knew that a little gun was hidden in a drawer in the sitting room. While the search was ongoing, she pitched the gun out the back window into the garden. She was unsure if the officer in charge had seen the gun, but he brought her out to the garden, where he admired the currant bushes and flowers. She could see the gun on the ground and he looked at her and said, "Am I seeing something I shouldn't see?" She did not reply as she was terror stricken and shaking in fear. He moved over to where the gun lay, and put his foot on it, pushing it into the earth, so that it would be hidden from the view of his colleagues. Without another word he and his men left and, "he saw her and she saw him for the last time." She never had any trouble afterwards and later, when the Truce came about, her husband returned home and began to build up his business again. He was not actively involved in politics but it was always expected of him to bring along his truck at election time, and to speak. He was a great supporter of de Valera, and a man of great influence in the locality.

As I was leaving, Rory Sweeney promised that one day soon he would bring me to The Cashen near Ballyduff to take a look at the ruins of the old family home and the creamery where acts of destruction and mayhem, and one act of great humanity took place in bygone troubled days.

Eily O'Flaherty and comrade in arms.

Historical photograph taken from the album of Eily O'Flaherty

Historical photograph taken from the album of Eily O'Flaherty

Historical photograph taken from the album of Eily O'Flaherty

Origanal Republican monument at Clashmealcon, North Kerry

Republicans at Clashmealcon Caves, North Kerry

Historical photograph taken from the album of Eily O'Flaherty

Front left to right: Andy Moynihan, Thomas Murphy
Back left to right: Michael O'Donnell, James Murphy & Tom Batt O'Connor c. 1920

CD No. 26
Time: 64.21
Publisher: Maurice O'Keeffe. ©

In 2001, which was the year of his death, the family of the late Tom Batt O'Connor contacted me to suggest that his memories should be recorded, as he had some very interesting facts to relate about historical events in Kerry and he was now in the later years of his long life. I made immediate plans to meet him at his home in Glenagealt,

and despite his deafness, he was a most fascinating person to interview and to record.
Tom Batt was born in July 1907 and at four years of age he remembered the trauma
and excitement locally when the Tralee to Dingle train was blown off the tracks at
Camp in a gust of wind. He recalled the train journey to Tralee which he frequently
made, about the absolute necessity of the train service, and he recalled that ladies were
charged 3d for the trip from Camp to Tralee and men were allowed to travel free!

The train would always slow down at the Railway Bar in Camp for the agile among the
passengers to alight for refreshments, and on one memorable occasion he recalled local
man Jimmy O'Connor raising his voice to sing an old Fenian Ballad from earlier
historic days.

He clearly recalled hearing about the Rising in Dublin at Easter 1916, and he told me
that at that time in Camp, people involved with Sinn Féin would regularly make
Republican speeches. The speakers would duly be arrested and amongst them was local
man Teddy Cronin, who languished in jail for a year as a result of his oratory.

There were five RIC officers stationed at Camp, and some local wit composed a ditty
about these gentlemen which Tom had no hesitation in reciting for me:

"Buckley is a gentleman
Barney is a spy
Phelan is a traitor and a traitor he will die,
Not forgetting Shelbourne
And Burke is worst of all
He made the people shiver when he came from Annascaul."

When Tom Batt was thirteen years old, he recalled one day seeing trenches which had
been dug across the roads on both the Tralee and Castlegregory sides of the village of
Camp. There were also sandbags in evidence near the RIC barracks and it was obvious
that something was afoot. That night, the shooting started and continued all night.
The IRA had planted a bomb up the chimney in the barracks, but as it was poorly
positioned, it succeeded merely in blowing a hole in the outer wall. Towards morning,
the firing ceased and the RIC men made good their escape to Tralee, and did not return
to their barracks in Camp again.

The O'Connor home in Glenagealt was a safe house for the IRA during the Civil War,
and it was a busy house during those years. One occasion stayed in Tom Batt's memory.
He vividly recalled an IRA man helping his father to pick potatoes, and having spotted
the Free State Forces approach instantly gathered his meagre belongings and was gone
in seconds.

Tom Batt had many fascinating details and events to relate about the years 1916 to
1923 and I am very glad that I was afforded the opportunity to interview this
marvellous raconteur prior to his death which occurred shortly after the recording was
made.

The Late Tom Batt O'Connor, Glenagealt, Co. Kerry

The late Maurice Barrett, Castleisland, Co. Kerry

CD No. 27

Time: 40.18

Publisher: Maurice O'Keeffe. ©

In the summer of 2000, I was searching out a house in the locality of Scartaglin, Co Kerry, when I stopped to ask directions at an old cottage with an open front door. Maurice Barrett was sitting inside by the fire, and I was invited to come in and sit down, which I did. It was not long before it became obvious that I should get my recording equipment from the car, because before me was a man with recollections rich and rare.

Maurice Barrett was born in Limerick in 1913, and shortly afterwards his father, who had been working in the mines in England, met a tragic death. At the age of three years his mother brought Maurice back to her home place at Castleisland.

He remembered and described the real fear he felt while going and coming from school in case the Black and Tans would pass him on the road, as "they were lawless and drunk day and night." He recalled a terrible day when two Black and Tans came to the house searching for Republicans. They were armed with rifles with bayonets, and they proceeded to ransack the house, stabbing the bayonets into the beds in their search.

He recalled Agent Sam Hussey of Edenburn House, Ballymacelligott, who was under constant guard by RIC in case of attack, and he also mentioned Lord Herbert of Currow who was shot in 1882 in earlier troubled days. In May 2005, I was sad to hear that this fine gentleman had passed away.

Una Sayers (Keane) c.1926

Una Keane, Ballyferriter, Co. Kerry

Ballyferriter is the birthplace of Una Keane, who is now 95 years old. She resides at Ocean View Nursing Home at Camp, near Tralee. When I met her in 2004 she told me she spend her younger days in the lovely village of Ballyferriter in West Kerry, and went on to describe for me an incident which has remained etched in her memory from those far off days.

When she was about ten years old, she would often see the Auxiliaries' lorries on the roads around the village and on the occasion of a meitheal at her home place, she and her mother were bringing tea to the men in the fields. As they walked along the road, a lorry of Auxiliaries appeared, and a flock of geese scattered ahead of the lorry. One of the British picked up his gun and aimed and fired at one of the geese, killing it, before driving off leaving mother and daughter traumatised and distressed, and as Una told the story it was obvious that she could still see in her mind's eye that occasion of mindless violence on a country road so long ago.

Frank Blennerhassett, Tralee, Co. Kerry

Frank Blennerhassett of Tralee is now in his 90th year and as I have had occasion to record his memories in the past, I was determined to visit him again, to sit and listed to his recollections of earlier days in Tralee.

He was born into a Church of Ireland family of farmers at Ballymacelligott about four miles from Tralee town. As a child he vividly remembers a group of three Volunteers passing through the farmyard, armed with rifles, and a day or two later four others arrived demanding a meal and a bed for the night.

He also recalls that about this time a very popular teacher in the locality, a Mr Flahive, was travelling one day by pony and trap, and as the nearest bridge had been blown up, he diverted to a temporary bridge at Ballycarty. The pony took fright whilst crossing the bridge, and Mr Flahive fell into the river and was drowned, an innocent victim of the troubles.

Another local incident recalled was the occasion when two youths named of Leen and Reidy, who were on the wanted list, were sitting in a house at Ballydwyer, when the door burst open and they were shot by a Major McKinnon, who was later to meet his fate in Tralee.

One afternoon while coming from school, Frank stood to watch a small plane, the first he'd ever seen, fly low over his house. It was a single engine, double wing plane, bearing the remains of Major McKinnon who had been shot and killed by a sniper at the old golf course at Tralee on the previous day.

Shortly before the Civil War began, Frank Blennerhassett's father had purchased some land from Major Chute of Chutehall, close to the Blennerhassett farm. Some of their neighbours were unhappy at this purchase and a group of them, with four pairs of horses and a mowing machine, cut the hay on the land, and carted it away to a farm about two miles away. Eventually the hay was sold and the proceeds enjoyed by the neighbours. On another occasion, the Blennerhassett cattle were driven off the land, and sent in the direction of Lyrecompane, so Mr Blennerhassett had to get on horseback and go and round up his cattle and get them home

When the Civil War ended, he made a complaint to the new Garda Siochána, and those involved were arrested and charged, and Mr Blennerhassett was awarded damages and costs. Some people locally felt very embittered at this turn of events, but as time went by most of those were reconciled with the Blennerhassett family and would gather at the house to listen to football matches on the radio, or to help out with the harvest.

Mr Blennerhassett is a fascinating man with an excellent memory for days long gone and I was very happy to be in his company and to listen to his recollections of historic events in Tralee.

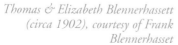

Thomas & Elizabeth Blennerhassett (circa 1902), courtesy of Frank Blennerhasset

Michael Howard, Kilrush, Co Clare

CD No. 28

Time:

Publisher: Maurice O'Keeffe. ©

In early April 2005, I was invited to Knockerra National School in Co Clare to record local resident Michael Howard, as he spoke to the children of the school and answered their many questions on local history. Several of the children were curious about events which occured during the years 1916 to 1923 and as Michael answered their questions, I decided that I would visit his home to record his memories of those historic days in Co Clare.

A few weeks later, I made my way to Tarmon, near Kilrush, where Michael lives in a cottage which has been in the Howard family for four generations – "A great IRA house" as Michael said.

He was born in November 1915 and he has a clear memory of groups of men gathering regularly in his house in 1921, before and after a skirmish, and he would sit fascinated to listen to the planning and organising and the discussion of recent guerrilla activities. There was always a scout posted on the road nearby watching out for the military, but as he lived in a very quiet and rural area, the trucks could be heard to approach well in advance of their arrival. On one occasion there were thirty men in the house when the trucks were heard on the road, and there was a general scramble out the back door.

Michael named out the local IRA members who were active in the area and who would frequent his house, and on three occasions the Black and Tans came to the house and put the family out in preparation for the burning of the property, but the burning never actually took place. A nearby house owned by the O'Donnell family was used by Eamon de Valera several times as a safe house, and in later years, when he was in the area, he would always pay a visit.

The Kilrush Ambush of 1921 was recalled in stirring tones in a fine recitation written by Jack O'Donnell who was a first cousin of the patriot Con Colbert.

I enquired of Michael if he had been acquainted with Garda Superintendent William Geary, who was stationed in Kilrush from 1926 to 1928, and who was dismissed from the Force in 1928 for allegedly taking a bribe of £100 from the IRA. Michael became quite animated at the mention of Superintendent Geary's name, and went on to tell me of several occurrences which contradict the recollections of William Geary whom I had previously recorded in the year of this death in New York in 2004.

Michael's father was a personal friend of Dan Breen of the Tipperary IRA, who wrote the famous book *My Fight for Irish Freedom*. Dan Breen once remarked to him that if he could have foretold the way things would go "he would never have fired a shot."

Michael recalled for me an extraordinary occurrence from August 1924 when Eamon de Valera came to Ennis, and was arrested and brought to the barracks. A situation arose which came to involve the Catholic Bishop of Clare, Dr Fogarty and William T Cosgrave in Dublin.

Michael recounted a story told to him by his father, concerning events in Kilrush during the occupation of the town by the Black and Tans. Mr Howard was involved with the Volunteers and he was acquainted with a Tan in Kilrush who would tell him when a raid was due to happen and that Tan could walk around the town at 10 o'clock at night and "he wouldn't be touched – the boys knew him"

Michael Howard's wonderfully clear memories of local historical events in Kilrush were a joy to record, and I made a promise to him before leaving that I would return one day soon to sit and reminisce with him once again.

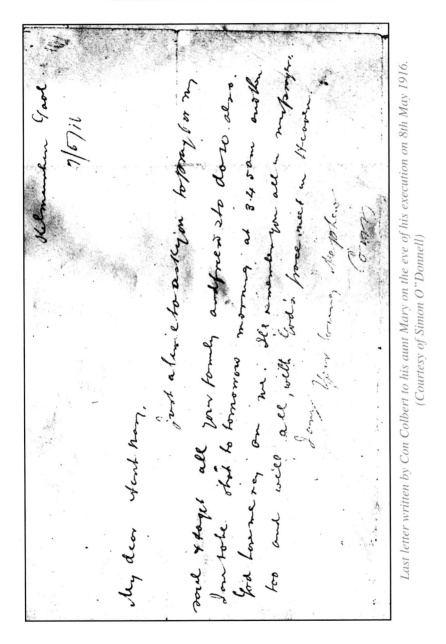

Last letter written by Con Colbert to his aunt Mary on the eve of his execution on 8th May 1916.

(Courtesy of Simon O'Donnell)

Diarmuid Mullins, Broadford, Co. Limerick

CD No. 29

Time: 50.29

Publisher: Maurice O'Keeffe. ©

In April 2002 I called to the home of Mrs Peggy Lynch Lyne in Killarney and as we chatted, I spotted a framed photograph of Liam Lynch, Chief of Staff, IRA, who was shot during the Civil War in 1923. Peggy told me that Liam Lynch was her uncle, brother to her father Jack. She told me that she had in her possession some twenty seven letters written by Liam Lynch during the years 1917 to 1923. She had always treasured these letters and generously allowed me access to them, and I was very pleased to sit and study these beautifully written letters which Liam Lynch penned to his mother at home in Fermoy and to his brother Tom, a priest working in Australia. He had always been very close to Tom and as I read the letters I got the feeling that here was a man who wanted to recount his experiences of guerilla warfare, and who felt he could do so openly to his dearly loved brother Tom.

As these letters had been treasured within the family, and had not previously been seen in public, I suggested to Peggy that she might consider allowing historians and academics to have access to them.

After some discussion it was decided that I would bring the letters to Dr Noel Kissane at the National Library in Dublin with a view to having them placed there, and happily they are now in the Library where they can be accessed and studied, and a brighter light can be shone on a complex and brave individual who sacrificed his life in Ireland's cause.

Before the letters left the house in Killarney, I sat down with Peggy Lynch Lyne and a friend of mine, avid historian Liam Lynch from Knocknagoshel, and we recorded aspects of the life of the patriot, and Peggy read passages from his fascinating and truly historical letters. This recording, from 2002, now forms part of the "Irish Life and Lore" collections of recordings.

In April 2005 I travelled to Broadford, Co Limerick to meet a nephew of Liam Lynch, Diarmuid Mullins, who was introduced to me by his cousin Peggy. We initially discussed Diarmuid's family history and his childhood years in Fermoy. He was two years old when his uncle Liam was shot and he recounted for me his uncle's involvement in the very beginning of the War of Independence. Fermoy was a garrison town, and each Sunday, fifteen members of the military, fully armed, would attend service at the local church. Liam Lynch sought permission from GHQ to attack the soldiers and seize their weapons, but initially permission was refused. Liam Lynch persisted and eventually permission was granted on condition that there was no bloodshed. The Volunteers armed themselves with batons and a few revolvers and the following Sunday they succeeded in relieving the military of fifteen rifles. One soldier was shot and wounded during the operation.

I enquired of Diarmuid if his uncle had had any involvement in the 1916 Rising, and he told me about a local man Donnacha O'Hannagáin from Anglesboro, Fermoy, who was in the GPO in 1916, but who escaped and went on the run in the area around his native place. Liam Lynch met up with him and invited him to his house, where they would discuss matters long into the night.

Diarmuid then read from a letter written by his uncle to Fr Tom Lynch in Australia in August 1921, where he recounts his experience of being under arrest a month after the Truce. He wrote, "I demanded the right as an Irish Army Officer to my own transport without an enemy permit as well as they do without our permits. I was released with my car driver after a phone message from Dublin Castle."

A letter written in July 1923 by Frank Aiken, Chief of Staff IRA to Fr Tom Lynch, was discussed. This letter is harrowing as it sets out the circumstances of Liam Lynch's shooting and its aftermath and is an important eyewitness account of the events of that grim day.

Diarmuid made a strong case for the vital work undertaken by the women of Cummann na mBan during those troubled years. He recalled the famous Clonbannin Ambush in North Cork, in which about fifty Corkmen and fifty Kerrymen took part. They had all previously walked about thirty miles to the ambush site. All of these men had to be fed, and as the fighting lasted all day, several meals had to be organised, and brought to the men. Breakfast was porridge and tea, dinner was bacon, spuds and cabbage, all of which disappeared in a flash. The women were taken by surprise by the fact that the fighting was still in progress at evening so they went home and baked bread for the next meal, but did not have any other provisions on hand, so they loaded

Liam Lynch, Chief of Staff, IRA

buckets with eggs, and brought them to the men, with the bread and the tea.

Diarmuid recalled an old soldier telling him that the best meal he had ever tasted was at Clonbannin where at tea time on the day of the ambush he feasted on tea, freshly baked bread and raw eggs!

Before we finished one recording I enquired of Diarmuid if he felt that his uncle had written the detailed letters we had discussed, in order to have his personal account on record, and Diarmuid pointed out that Liam had said "... if the worst happens, I'll have someone detailed to report it."

I am most grateful to Peggy Lynch Lyne and to Diarmuid Mullins for allowing me to record their family history and for bringing the spirit of their uncle Liam Lynch, so vividly to life for me.

Irish Republican Army

Field General Headquarters,

Dept..................
Ref. No..............

..............16 / 9 / 192 2.

Dear Tom.

    I have been very anxious for some time past to drop a note to you, so am pleased to have got present opportunity. I was afraid I could not meet you before you left Ireland on your long mission to Australia, but now I had hopes of seeing you in the near future. Reaver may perhaps be able to arrange when I can see you.

    The disaster of this war is sinking to my very bones when I count the loss of Irishmanhood & the general havoc of civil war. We have set ourselves to the task and if necessary will fight to the bitter end before we allow the nation dishonour itself.

    The I. R. A., most of whose members had already done most in the successful war against the common enemy, have now been hopelessly let down by their former comrades & leaders. It is bad enough they being formerly of I. R. A. if they only fought us clean, but they have stooped to lower methods than the British, including murder gangs with propaganda. I do hope I shall live through this that further generations will have written for them the full details of all the traitorous acts. Who could have dreamt that all our hopes could have been so blighted.

    M'Callaghan, Curraglass, Charleville – Thavie student – has been asking for you recently.

    Hoping Mother & all are well at home.

        Your fond brother,
        Liam Lynch.

Letter dated 16th September 1922 written by Liam Lynch to his brother Tom.

Lombardstown,
22/8/21.

Dear Tom.

It just struck me to change my war mind for a few minutes & think of home & surroundings & write to you. I hope you are enjoying your hollidays especially this year that truce is on

We had the C/S here for a week & the President for three days. We had a big tour of area when Coys & Columns — under arms & equipment — were inspected. I assure you, we were delighted with them especially our visitors. We went through all war zone & visited several ambush positions.

By the way I was in jail last Thursday from 6 P.M to 1.30 A.M, was arrested near Ballinhassig by 3 cars of Black & Tans & a D.I & taken back to Bandon. I demanded the right as an Irish Army Officer to use my own transport without an enemy permit, as well as they do without our permits. I was released with my car & driver at 1.30 a.m. after a phone message from Dublin Castle as both our peoples had previously been in touch in Cork on the matter. I enjoyed the time with Tans. & D. I. etc as the Truce feeling prevailed all round & we discussed the possibility of again meeting them face to face in a clash with arms.

Hope this truce will last some time as I am anxious to get a few more days at home.

You can write or post to me enclosing letter in envelope marked with my own name & personal to :— Miss Mary Looney, Gortmore, Lombardstown. Do you remember that last letter I wrote home, was it delivered.

Hope all at home are A1.   your fond brother,
                                              Liam.

Letter dated 22nd August 1921, written by Liam Lynch to his brother Tom, detailing his arrest by the black and tans near ballinhassig, Co. Cork

Officers of the First Southern Division, Irish Republican Army, attending Army Convention, at the Mansion House, Dublin 9, 9th April 1922. Front from left: Sean Lehane, Thomas Daly, Florrie O'Donoghue, Liam Lynch, Liam Deasy, Sean Moylan, John Joe Rice, Humphrey Murphy; second row: Dinny Daly, Jim O'Mahony, George Power, Mick Murphy, Eugen O'Neill, Sean McSwiney, Patrick O'Sullivan, Jim Murphy, Moss Donegan, Jerry Hanafin, third row: Jeremy O'Riordan, Mick Crowley, Dan Shinnick, Con Liddy, Con O'Leary, Tom Hales, Jack O'Neill, Sean McCarthy, Dick Barrett, Andy Cooney, fourth row: Sean Lordan, Gibbs Ross, Tadhg Brosnan, Dam Mulvihill, Denis McNeilus, at rear: Garret McAuliff, Con Casey, Pax Whelan, Tom McEllistrim, Michael Harrington

Diarmuid Ring, Valentia, Co. Kerry

CD No. 30
Time: 42.10
Publisher: Maurice O'Keeffe. ©

One fine autumn day in 2004, I drove to Valentia Island to meet cousins Diarmuid and Owen Ring, sons of the famous Ring brothers, Tim and Eugene, who were responsible for alerting American and Germany to the fact that Ireland had risen in arms at Easter 1916. The following April I decided that another trip to Valentia would be very worthwhile, so one Sunday morning I turned up once again at the home of Diarmuid Ring, only to find that he was at Mass. I took a stroll while I waited and on his return, Diarmuid was happy to see me again, and to offer his time and his recollections of a family of renown which has always been steeped in national pride.

Diarmuid's great grandfather, Tadgh Ring, was born at a place called Kilmurray outside Kenmare and became a schoolteacher at Cullen in North Cork. In 1865, when a Fenian Rising was planned he closed the school, armed himself and marched to Killarney to meet up with the Iveragh Fenians. The Rising was aborted, and on his return to Cullen was dismissed from his post at the school by the parish priest who disapproved of his extra curricular activities.

Tadgh Ring's son Jerry, who was Diarmuid's grandfather worked at the post office in Cork as a telegraphist, and later applied for a position as a cable operator on Valentia in 1875. He married a local girl, Sarah Cremin, and they got a house on the island from the cable company.

Tim, their son, and father of Diarmuid, grew up on the island and joined the IRB. He

Tim Ring c. 1915

lived in a room over the cable station, and after the Rising of 1916, his room was raided by the British and they found, amongst other things, a copy of John Mitchell's "Jail Journal" which they felt was highly incriminating. The telegraph sent to John Devoy in America about the Rising had been traced to the Ring brothers, so both Tim and his brother Eugene were arrested, and Tim was incarcerated in Frongoch prison in North Wales.

Some years ago Diarmuid Ring, suspecting that a file would have been kept on his father Tim by the British authorities after 1916, began a search in the National Archives and there he found that his suspicions were correct. He read for me a letter from the file, written to the Chief Secretary's Office and dated 4th November 1916.

"Timothy Ring is without doubt a disloyal and dangerous man. He is well educated and used his position as cable operator, at Valentia, to send a telegram to America which gave information on the outbreak in April. His explanation of this telegram, which is recorded in the file which is now at the Home Office, was so unsatisfactory as to be incredible. In my opinion he should not be allowed return to Ireland at all. If this is done, it is only a question of time when further representations will be made to have him restored to his position in the cable station and the fact that other members of his family are still there will make it an easy matter for him to resume his attempts to evade the censorship, whether he is reemployed or not. If, however, it is decided to release him, provided he enters into an undertaking with sureties for his good behaviour, I have no objection to offer, and hope that the undertaking will be made as stringent as possible."

Signed Maxwell,
General Commanding in Chief – The Forces in Ireland,
Headquarters Irish Command
Parkgate,
Dublin.

Diarmuid read some further historical letters from the file, and told me that his father spoke little in his later years about his time in London, after his release from Frongoch in 1917. After Tim Ring's death, Diarmuid was told by a local man, J. J. Kelly whose pen name was "Sceilig" that Tim had still been involved in Ireland's cause while he lived in London. In 1918, during the Great War, there was a possibility that conscription might be introduced in Ireland and Cathal Brugha was sent to London in an attempt to prevent this. There was a plan to smuggle a weapon into the House of Commons, and Tim Ring went and checked the place to decide what type of weapon should be smuggled in. In the event nothing came of this plan, as the war came to an end shortly thereafter.

That Sunday drive to Valentia in April 2005 was a fascinating interlude and a true glimpse into a life lived to the full in troubled times in a troubled Ireland.

1622 (A.-2.)

CHIEF SECRETARY.

TIMOTHY RING is without doubt a disloyal and
dangerous man. He is well educated and used his position as
Cable Operator at Valentia to send a telegram to America which
gave information regarding the outbreak in April.   His explanation of this telegram, which is recorded in the file
which is now at the Home Office, was so unsatisfactory as to
be incredible.   In my opinion he should not be allowed to
return to Ireland at all.   If this is done it is only a
question of time when further representations will be made
to have him restored to his position in the Cable Station,
and the fact that other members of his family are still there
will make it an easy matter for him to resume his attempts
to evade the censorship, whether he is re-employed or not.

If, however, it is decided to release him provided
he enters into ~~finishing~~ an undertaking with Sureties for his
good behaviour, I have no objection to offer, and hope that
the undertaking will be made as stringent as possible.

                              General,
                    Commanding-in-Chief the Forces in

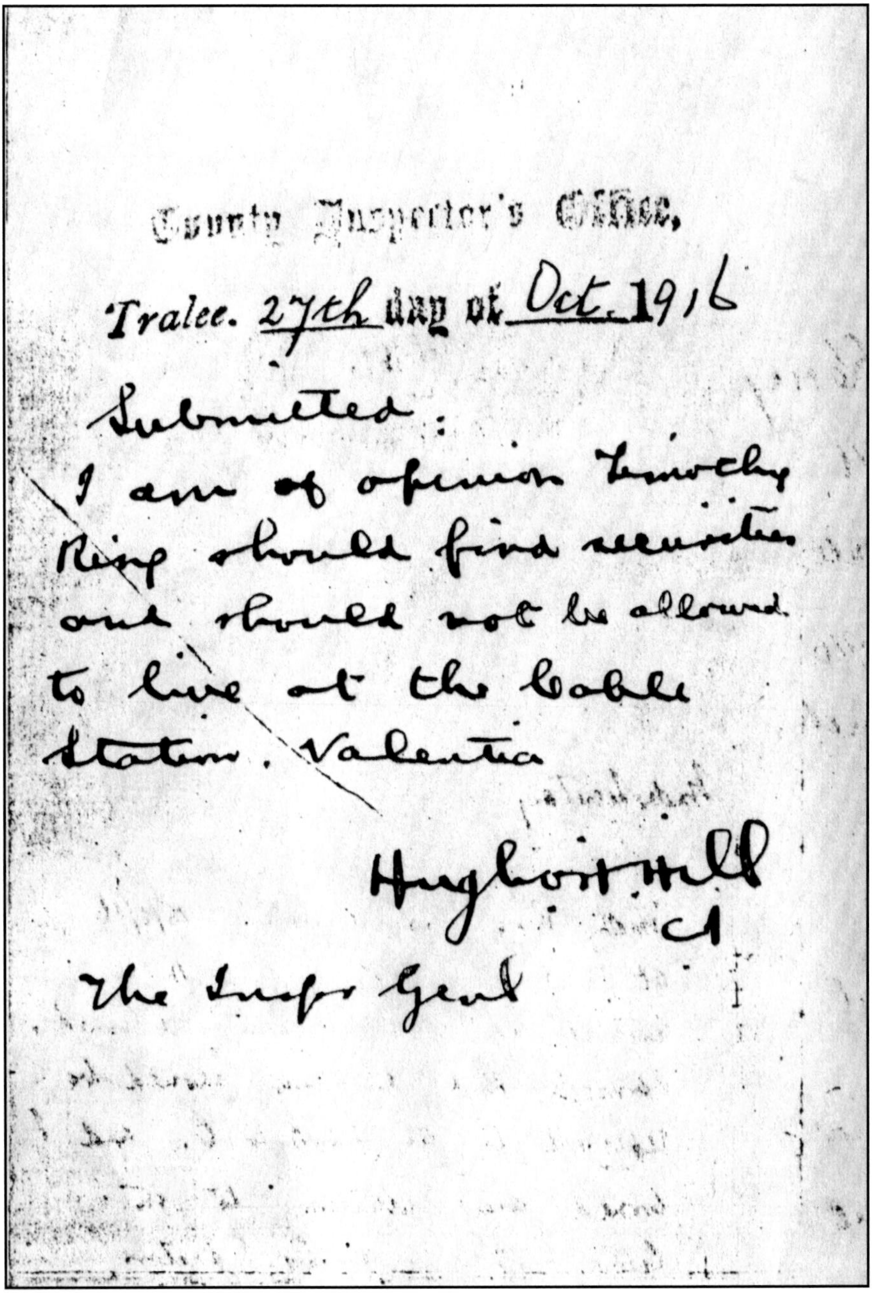

County Inspector's Office,

Tralee. 27th day of Oct. 1916

Submitted :
I am of opinion Timothy
Ring should find securities
and should not be allowed
to live at the Cable
Station. Valentia

Hugh o't Hill
cl

The Insp. Genl

22889

12th December 1916.

Sir,

In reply to your letter of the 2nd instant (321,143/3), respecting the case of interned Irish prisoner TIMOTHY RING, I have to acquaint you, for the information of the Secretary of State, that the application for this man's release was made direct to the Chief Secretary by the Hon. Mrs Spring Rice, and that the Irish Government do not consider that Ring should be released unless he can be excluded from Ireland.

I am,

Sir,

Your obedient Servant,

t.o.3

The Under Secretary of State,
Home Office,
London, S.W.

Valentia cable station, office and dwelling blocks. (courtesy of Diarmuid ing)